T0012309

ATHLETES FOR
SOCIAL
JUSTICE

COLIN KAEPERNICK, LEBRON JAMES, AND MORE

by Dolores Andral

CAPSTONE PRESS
a capstone imprint

Published by Capstone Press, an imprint of Capstone.
1710 Roe Crest Drive, North Mankato, Minnesota 56003
capstonepub.com

Library of Congress Cataloging-in-Publication Data
Names: Andral, Dolores, author.
Title: Athletes for social justice : Colin Kaepernick, Lebron James, and more / by
Dolores Andral.
Description: North Mankato, Minnesota : Capstone Press, [2022] | Series: Sports
illustrated kids: activist athletes | Includes bibliographical references and index.
| Audience: Ages 8-11 | Audience: Grades 4-6 | Summary: "Taking a stand and
being an activist means having the courage to speak up for an important cause.
For football player Colin Kaepernick and basketball great LeBron James, fighting
for social justice is their top priority. Learn how they and other players use their
platform as celebrity athletes to bring attention and change to the cause of social
justice"— Provided by publisher.
Identifiers: LCCN 2021030713 (print) | LCCN 2021030714 (ebook) | ISBN
9781663965981 (hardcover) | ISBN 9781666321418 (paperback) | ISBN
9781666321425 (pdf) | ISBN 9781666321449 (kindle edition)
Subjects: LCSH: Athletes—Political activity—Juvenile literature. | Social justice—
Juvenile literature.
Classification: LCC GV706.35 .A63 2022 (print) | LCC GV706.35 (ebook) | DDC
796.092/2 [B]—dc23
LC record available at https://lccn.loc.gov/2021030713
LC ebook record available at https://lccn.loc.gov/2021030714

Image Credits
AP Photo: File, 5, Frank Franklin II, top, Seth Wenig, 11, Nick Wass, 9, Vincent
Thian, 19; Curtis Compton: Atlanta Journal-Constitution via AP, 17; Getty
Images: JP Yim/Contributor, 21, Julio Aguilar, 27, Mike Ehrmann/Staff, 29; Mike
Ehrmann: Pool Photo via AP, 28; Mo Khursheed: TFV Media via AP Images, 12;
Newscom: CNP/Polaris, 13, EFE/Ricardo Maldonado Rozo, 20, Icon SMI/Mark
Halmas, 14, Icon Sportswire/Nick Wosika, 16, Reuters/Jessica Rinaldi, 15, TNS/
Nhat V. Meyer, 7; Shutterstock: AlexanderTrou, Cover; Sports Illustrated: Al
Tielemans, 24, Bob Martin, 23, Erick W. Rasco, 25

Editorial Credits
Editor: Erika L. Shores; Designer: Heidi Thompson; Media Researcher: Jo Miller;
Production Specialist: Tori Abraham

TABLE OF CONTENTS

Words in BOLD appear in the glossary.

INTRODUCTION

Shout. Sit. Raise fists. People have always found ways to fight unfair treatment. Athletes are no different. Pro athletes are often seen as superstars. Some of them use their star power to fight for social justice.

Social justice means bringing equality to all. Everyone has the right to a good education, fair pay, health care, and safety. How much money a person has, their skin color, or their gender should not matter.

Famous athletes use many ways to spread their messages of social justice. They kneel, tweet, or put their message on a shirt. Their messages reach people around the world.

FAMOUS PROTEST

Tommie Smith and John Carlos were two Black American athletes. They won medals during the 1968 Olympics. The men wore black gloves and raised their fists during the medal ceremony. They were silently protesting the **racism** Black people faced in the United States. Peter Norman, a white Australian athlete, joined the protest by wearing a badge. It showed a group's name that fought against racism.

Australian Peter Norman (left), U.S. athlete Tommie Smith (center), and U.S. athlete John Carlos (right) on the Olympic podium in 1968

TAKING A STAND

One important social issue involves **policing** in Black communities. Famous athletes have made their opinions known about police **brutality**. They bring attention to the harsh and sometimes deadly treatment of Black people by the police.

COLIN KAEPERNICK

Colin Kaepernick was an American football player with the San Francisco 49ers. Beginning in 2016, he kneeled during the national anthem. He wanted to draw attention to the mistreatment of Black people by the police.

The way Kaepernick protested got a lot of **backlash**. Some Americans felt he did not respect the U.S. flag or the country. But Kaepernick never intended that to be his message. He hoped to shine a light on an ongoing problem.

Many athletes and **activists** from around the world supported Kaepernick. He kept speaking out even after no NFL team would sign him to a new contract. He believed what he was doing was more important than football.

Eli Harold (left) and Eric Reid (right) joined Colin Kaepernick (center) in kneeling during the national anthem before a game on October 2, 2016.

THE DEATH OF GEORGE FLOYD

In 2020, George Floyd, an unarmed Black man, was killed by the police in Minneapolis. Officer Derek Chauvin kneeled on Floyd's neck for more than nine minutes. Floyd's death sparked outrage around the world. Protests happened in all 50 states, more than 60 countries, and on all seven continents. Many people who had not supported Kaepernick changed their views. Head of the National Football League (NFL), Commissioner Roger Goodell, even apologized to Kaepernick.

GEORGE HILL AND THE MILWAUKEE BUCKS

Basketball player George Hill was a point guard for the Milwaukee Bucks in 2020. A global **pandemic** meant National Basketball Association (NBA) players had to live in a "bubble." That meant they had to avoid places that could expose them to the COVID-19 virus. But Hill wanted to join the protests for racial justice.

Hill found his own way. He decided not to take part in a playoff game. "There's bigger issues and bigger things to tackle in life right now than a basketball game," he said.

The entire Bucks team decided to join Hill. They planned to **boycott** Game 5 of the playoffs. After the Bucks' decision, the NBA decided to postpone the other playoff games that day.

FACT

The shooting of Jacob Blake, a 29-year-old Black man from Kenosha, Wisconsin, by a police officer caused Hill and the NBA to boycott a game. Other sports leagues followed, including the Women's National Basketball Association (WNBA), Major League Baseball (MLB), and the National Hockey League (NHL). The NFL canceled practices.

George Hill led the way for other pro athletes and teams to protest for social justice.

NAOMI OSAKA

After winning her first U.S. Open in 2018, tennis star Naomi Osaka became the highest paid female athlete. But Osaka could not ignore the deaths of unarmed Black people by police.

The global pandemic in 2020 caused people to wear masks in public. There are seven rounds of the U.S. Open. During each round, Osaka wore a mask with the name of a different Black American who was killed in a situation of police violence or racial profiling. One victim was named Breonna Taylor. Taylor was asleep in her home when police barged in and shot her.

Osaka also spoke out against violence toward Asian people. Some people falsely blamed Chinese people for the spread of the COVID-19 virus. Osaka called for people to love Asians as much as they love Asian products, entertainment, and culture.

Four of the masks Naomi Osaka wore in 2020

COMING OUT FOR SOCIAL JUSTICE

Social justice means equal rights for all. Members of the **LGBTQIA+** community have had to fight for rights, such as marrying who they want. Athletes who are part of this community share their personal stories to make a difference.

MEGAN RAPINOE

Megan Rapinoe helped the U.S. Women's Soccer Team win two Women's World Cups. The team also won a gold medal at the 2012 Summer Olympics. Rapinoe fought for equality for Black people and equal pay for women. She also fought for LGBTQIA+ rights.

Soccer star Megan Rapinoe during a 2015 match

Rapinoe became the first female soccer player to come out publicly as gay. Rapinoe used her fame to carve a path for gay athletes in sports. In a book she wrote, she said, "I was proud to have spoken up in some small way. I felt like I was part of something bigger than myself."

In 2021, Megan Rapinoe spoke at the White House about equal pay for women.

JASON COLLINS

Jason Collins played in the NBA for 13 years. It shocked many people when he appeared on the cover of a 2013 *Sports Illustrated* titled: "The Gay Athlete." But even before coming out, he had been practicing his own kind of activism.

When Collins played for the Boston Celtics, he wore jersey number 98. He chose that number to honor Matthew Shepard. In 1998, Shepard was a student at the University of Wyoming. The 21-year-old was murdered because he was gay. Later, when Collins signed with the Brooklyn Nets, he again wore the number 98.

Jason Collins's jersey number was one way the NBA star quietly supported the LGBTQIA+ community.

Collins and his twin brother Jarron host summer basketball camps. Collins signaled support again with what he wore. He chose bright, rainbow-colored sneakers. It was one way to show that he accepted everyone.

Jason Collins took his activism to the streets by marching in Boston's Gay Pride Parade.

People have different reasons for speaking up. Some people choose to take a stand. Other people or groups have no choice.

MAJOR LEAGUE BASEBALL

Before 2020, MLB players had been fairly quiet about protesting for social justice. In 2010, when an immigration law was passed, the players thought about boycotting the 2011 All-Star Game. In the end, none of them did. However, in 2020, other sports leagues decided to boycott games after the shooting of Jacob Blake. MLB felt pressured to join them.

Signs at Miller Park displayed "Justice Equality Now" after the shooting of Jacob Blake in Wisconsin. Miller Park is home to the Milwaukee Brewers MLB team.

In 2021, MLB made headlines again. Georgia's governor passed a voting law. Many people worried that this law would make it harder for some people to vote. MLB decided to move the All-Star Game and **draft** out of Georgia in protest. MLB's commissioner spoke out saying the league supports voting rights for all Americans.

MLB fans show their support for the decision to move the All-Star Game out of Georgia.

IBTIHAJ MUHAMMAD

Pro **fencer** Ibtihaj Muhammad represented the United States at the 2016 Summer Olympics. She was the first **hijab**-wearing **Muslim** woman to do so. Muhammad knew she stood out as a Muslim who wore a hijab. She used the focus on her to do something powerful. She helped create Athletes for Impact. The group helps pro athletes get involved in activism. Muhammad helps athletes find groups to work with on social justice issues.

Muhammad also spoke out against issues such as the U.S. travel ban. People from the countries on the banned list could not enter the United States. Many of these countries have a large number of Muslim people living there. Muhammad knew what it was like to be singled out.

Ibtihaj Muhammad won a bronze medal during the 2016 Olympics.

MINDA DENTLER

Minda Dentler was the first female wheelchair athlete to complete the Ironman World Championship triathlon. As a child in India, Dentler became sick with polio. The disease left her unable to use her legs.

Dentler used her star power to bring attention to the need for medical care in India. She raised awareness about polio. She worked to help the millions of children who still suffer from it. In 2015, she traveled to India for National Immunization Day. The community where she was born still needed access to the polio vaccine. Around the country, 172 million children received the vaccine.

Minda Dentler handcycling in the Ironman World triathlon

Minda Dentler spoke about her work to end polio in India at an event in 2017.

EQUAL PAY AND EQUAL PLAY

Women have fought for equality for a long time. One battle is the fight for equal pay. Another is the fight for equal recognition.

VENUS WILLIAMS

Venus Williams won the women's tennis singles Grand Slam in 2000 at Wimbledon. She was paid less than the men's singles champion. She decided to fight for equal pay. In 2006, Williams wrote a letter to Wimbledon officials. In 2007, she won the Wimbledon championship for the fourth time. This time she finally got the same prize money as the men's champion. "That was something we had been working on since the 1960s," says Williams. "It was long overdue."

In 2021, Williams wrote a piece for *Vogue* magazine. This time she wrote about the pay difference between men and women outside of sports.

Venus Williams in action during a match at Wimbledon in 2007

www.wimbledon.

FACT

In 1970, pro tennis star Billie Jean King pushed for equal pay in prize money for female tennis players. Three years later, the U.S. Open was the first major tournament to award equal money to the men's and women's winners.

SERENA WILLIAMS

Tennis great Serena Williams has many major titles and Olympic medals. But because of her gender, some people thought she couldn't be called the greatest athlete. People often called her the greatest *female* athlete. But when people talked about men, they called them the GOAT (Greatest of All Time). Williams argued that they didn't use "world's greatest male athlete." Williams wanted people to focus on her talent, not on her gender.

Serena Williams has fought to earn the same recognition as top male athletes.

Williams also spoke out about unequal treatment on the tennis court. Williams sometimes shouted if she didn't agree with a call. This could result in something called a code violation. But Williams said male tennis players were treated differently. They did not always get a violation, even if their outbursts were the same or worse than hers.

Serena Williams argues with an umpire about a call during a match.

GET OUT AND VOTE

There was a time when women and people who weren't white could not vote. Because of this, many people take their right to vote seriously. Activist athletes reach out to others to get them to vote too.

WNBA

Kelly Loeffler is an owner of the WNBA team the Atlanta Dream. Loeffler wanted the team to drop their support of the Black Lives Matter (BLM) movement. The movement supports Black people, gay people, and others. Many Dream players are Black and gay.

Loeffler ran for the U.S. Senate in 2020. WNBA players backed Raphael Warnock. He was running against her. Players wore T-shirts that read Vote Warnock. They used interviews to connect with voters. Their actions helped Warnock win a seat in the Senate.

WNBA star Sue Bird wore a Vote Warnock
T-shirt during a 2020 game.

LEBRON JAMES

LeBron James joined the NBA straight out of high school. He has taken center stage ever since. Up until 2012, James did not speak out much on social issues. That changed after a 17-year-old African American boy named Trayvon Martin was killed. "From that point on, I knew that my voice and my platform had to be used for more than just sports," he said.

LeBron James uses his fame to support Black Lives Matter.

LeBron James and his teammates wore shirts reminding their fans of the importance of voting.

James used his voice to call out police brutality. He called for major changes to policing. James knew voting for people who could make these changes was important. He started "More Than a Vote" to encourage people to vote and learn about important issues.

James and other athletes have shown that there are many ways to be an activist. Sit out, write, wear a mask. Athletes find both quiet and loud ways to fight for their communities.

GLOSSARY

activist (AK-tiv-ist)—a person who works for social or political change

backlash (BAK-lash)—a strong negative reaction to an issue

boycott (BOY-kaht)—to refuse to take part in something as a way of making a protest

brutality (broo-TAL-uh-tee)—cruel, harsh, and usually violent treatment of another person

draft (DRAFT)—an event in which athletes are picked to join sports organizations or teams

fencer (FEN-sur)—a person who practices the sport of fencing; fencing involves using swords

hijab (hi-JAHB)—a traditional covering for the hair and neck that is worn by Muslim women

LGBTQIA+—an abbreviation for the community that includes: Lesbian, Gay, Bisexual, Transgender, Queer, Intersex, Asexual, plus everything else

Muslim (MUHZ-luhm)—someone who follows the religion of Islam

pandemic (pan-DEM-ik)—a disease that spreads over a wide area and affects many people

policing (puh-LEESS-ing)—to control, regulate, or keep in order

racism (RAY-siz-uhm)—the belief that one race is better than another race

READ MORE

Easton, Emily. *Enough! 20 Protesters Who Changed America*. New York: Crown Books for Young Readers, 2018.

Hoena, Blake. *Colin Kaepernick: Athletes Who Made a Difference*. Minneapolis: Lerner Publishing Group, 2020.

Koya, Lena, and Laura La Bella. *Female Athletes*. New York: The Rosen Publishing Group, Inc., 2018.

INTERNET SITES

The LeBron James Family Foundation
lebronjamesfamilyfoundation.org/

Youth Activism Project
youthactivismproject.org/

Youth Civil Rights Academy: Sports for Social Justice
youthcivilrights.org/portfolio_page/sports-for-social-justice/

INDEX

ABOUT THE AUTHOR

Dolores Andral earned an MFA from Queens University in Charlotte, NC. She loves writing for kids because she believes children should see themselves reflected in the books they read. She lives with her husband and four kids in Washington State.